STEVE PARKER

Copyright © QED Publishing 2014

First published in the UK in 2014 by
QED Publishing
A Quarto Group company
230 City Road
London EC1V 2TT
www.qed-publishing.co.uk

A catalogue record for this book is available from the British Library.

ISBN 978 1 78171 163 7

Project Editor Carey Scott
Illustrator Peter David Scott/The Art Agency
Designer Dave Ball
QED Project Editor Tasha Percy
Managing Editor Victoria Garrard
Design Manager Anna Lubecka

Printed and bound in China

Photo Credits
Key: t = top, b = bottom, l = left, r = right, c = centre,
FC = front cover, BC = back cover.
Shutterstock Cathy Keifer 5tl, worldwildlifewonders 5tr, Eric Isselee 5bl,
de2marco 25b; **Corbis** Piotr Naskrecki/Minden Pictures 5br; Ocean 21; **Alamy**
FLPA 15b; **Nature Picture Library** Solvin Zanki 15t, Ross Hoddinott 18t

Contents

I'm at home in water – or out of it!

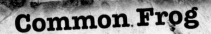

Common Frog

Group Amphibians – frogs and toads

Adult length 8 centimetres

Weight Up to 25 grammes

Habitat Ponds, streams, ditches, damp places

Food Flies and other insects, worms and slugs

Features Large eyes, long back legs, webbed back feet. Smooth, shiny skin that the frog can breathe through

Wake-up Time

Yawn. Stre-e-e-tch. Sh-sh-shake. At last my Cold Sleep is over. As my surroundings warm up, so do I. It seems as though four months have passed ... in fact, they have! But I'm still a young frog - just two years old. Future winters could be even longer and colder.

The bright sunlight makes me blink.

I've been well protected from the cold underneath the mud, moss, leaves, bark and twigs in My Den. I'll tidy it now, so it is ready for when I return next winter.

My leg muscles are still stiff.

Thick fur keeps Mouse warm and dry.

Mouse ran past, twitching her whiskers and sniffing for food. Being ~~worm-bludded~~ warm-blooded, she must stay active and eat every few hours just to stay alive. Last winter she nearly starved to death about six times!

WHAT IS AN AMPHIBIAN?

Amphibians are animals that live on land and in water. They are cold-blooded, so their body temperature changes with their surroundings. Amphibians lay eggs in water, which hatch into tadpoles. As they grow up, the tadpoles change shape greatly, which is called metamorphosis.

Main Groups

• Newts and salamanders have four legs and a tail.
• Frogs and toads have four legs but no tail.
• Caecilians have no legs and look like worms.

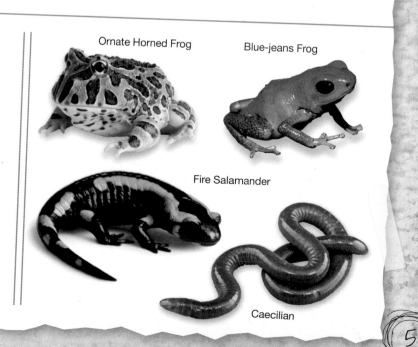

Ornate Horned Frog

Blue-jeans Frog

Fire Salamander

Caecilian

Dangerous Journey

Quickly I gobbled up a few worms and slugs. I need plenty of food because it's time to leave for Big Pond. It's an epic journey, full of hazards. At least I hope so, because I'm a frog who just loves excitement!

Before I leave My Den, I look carefully around for enemies like Fox or Heron. I usually travel at dusk, because they cannot see me so easily in the dim light.

Before setting off, I check for danger.

I leap super-quickly across the Hard Track.

Toad is also heading for Big Pond, but I'm faster.

Tree roots are a good place for hiding.

Whoa! I spy that rotter Otter on the opposite bank!

Safe at last in Big Pond!

6

Crossing the Hard Track is sooo exciting! I have to dodge the big, fast, noisy creatures with bright shining eyes. I wait until it's all quiet - then leap like crazy!

Heron can swoop past at any time.

Two-eyed Monsters are so fast!

Beware Fox, he's so clever!

Uh-oh! I spy Fox nosing along the riverbank. He would rather catch a big, warm, tasty rabbit than me, but in early spring, everyone is extra-hungry.

Uh-oh! I think Otter has seen me.

Otter

Group Mammals - carnivores

Length 70 centimetres, plus 40 centimetre tail

Weight 10-12 kilogrammes

Habitat Rivers, lakes, marshes, seashores

Food Fish, birds, water insects, crayfish, frogs (!)

Features Thick waterproof fur, long whiskers, webbed feet and long muscular tail for powerful swimming

Puff, pant, I'm almost at Big Pond. AARGH - Otter! If I take one last great jump, I can hide among the old lilies and waterweeds. Here I go - made it!

Big Pond

It's great to be back in the water, even if it's still quite chilly. Big Pond looks untidy after the winter. I hate mess. Maybe I'll clear out the old leaves and lumps of moss.

Common Newt

Group Amphibians – newts and salamanders

Length 8–10 centimetres, plus tail

Weight 2–3 grammes

Habitat Ponds, streams, ditches, damp places in woods and meadows

Food Insects, slugs, snails, tadpoles

Features Long tail, short legs, belly spots, male has a crest and bright colours when breeding

I'm slowly remembering my swimming skills.

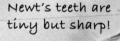

Newt's teeth are tiny but sharp!

Like me, Newt sleeps in a den during the winter. Now he's back. That means he's hungry too. Newt is OK, but there's a chance he might eat some of our tadpoles!

Backswimmer practises rowing.

Speedy the water snail stays in Big Pond during the winter, buried in the mud. That thick shell protects against enemies, and it looks so smart and neat. I do like tidy things!

Speedy's shell gets bigger each year.

04 MARCH

SPRING POND CHORES

- Remind myself of the shallow areas and deep parts.
- Check all my underwater hidey-holes are still there.
- Make sure Pike is not around this year.
- Learn a new swimming stroke – froggy paddle!

Roach feeds mainly in the mud.

Stickle's prickly spiky spines.

Fish like Roach and Stickle also spend winter in the water. Roach says they just lie on the bottom under the ice. Brrr! Stickle tells me that only seven sticklebacks survived the cold. The other nine died. How sad.

Catching Prey

I tidied my three main sitting spots, where I wait for prey. Then, it was one feast after another. The grasshopper kicked my mouth hard and the centipede bit, but hey, I laugh in the face of danger!

Back foot – five webbed toes to swim fast.

Here comes a fly, awesome! It's only a small snack, but it's a tasty one. I sit still and wait, and wait ... my super-sharp eyesight tracks the fly's every wing-flap.

I breathe partly through my skin.

My ears hear buzzes and croaks.

Short, propped-up front legs.

My eyes spot tiny movements.

Long, folded-up back legs.

Ready, steady, FLICK. My amazing tongue shoots out. It's almost half as long as me, and the fly sticks to its tip.

Favourite Foods

Here are some drawings of my all-time favourite foods. My sketches are getting quite good. I use waterproof ink, of course!

Moth

Earthworm

Mayfly

Damselfly

My tongue's all muscle!

Slime at the tip of my tongue traps the fly.

I pull in my tongue and swallow the fly in one gulp. Frogs have such tiny teeth that we cannot bite or chew our food into pieces. One swallow and it's gone, which is why our mouths are so wide. Big smile!

Front foot – four separated toes to land on after leaping.

Croak, Ribbet

Croak, wurp, rarp, ribbet. It's so noisy at this time of year! I'm too young to breed, so I don't get excited in spring, like grown-up frogs do. But I look and learn. Males are smaller and they croak. Females are bigger and they don't.

HOW TO CROAK

1. Breathe air into lungs.

2. Breathe out through voicebox in throat.

3. Blow out chin to make croak louder.

Toads are breeding too.

I'm leaping out of here!

Male grasps female under her front legs.

The male croaks attract females. If a male thinks he has a chance, he waddles near her. She might push him off or swim away. But often she finds him suitable and they get together.

Look and listen for partners.

The male climbs onto the female, grabs her around her armpits, and stays like this for a few days. Cousin Toad does the same. How gross!

Male holds onto partner.

Common Toad

Group Amphibians – frogs and toads

Length Male 8–10 centimetres, female 12–16 centimetres

Weight Male up to 40 grammes, female 80 grammes

Habitat Ponds, streams, woods, parks, gardens, outbuildings

Food Worms and slugs and insects including beetles and woodlice

Features Large eyes, lumpy skin that oozes poisonous fluid

A lily pad makes a good viewpoint.

Chin blows out like a balloon when croaking.

Ears listen out for rival males.

Jelly Babies

Each spawn clump has over 1000 eggs.

It's time for grown-up females to lay their ~~sporn~~ spawn. When laid, each egg is covered in thin, slippery jelly stuff. The jelly quickly soaks up water and thickens to protect the egg. Nifty!

Jelly swells in the water.

Each dot is a tiny egg.

Who eats Frogspawn?

Almost everyone! But female frogs lay so many, some tadpoles will almost certainly survive and grow to become adult frogs.

Hedgehog nibbles spawn from near the bank.

Coot pecks at spawn from above.

Young tadpoles just fit into Newt's mouth.

Carp swallows lots with each gulp.

After a few days, the dots grow bigger and are called embryos. A few days later, each one develops a wiggly tail and starts to become a tadpole.

Toad's spawn is not a big clump, but long and winding, like string. She calls it her 'necklace'.

I remember being a tiny tadpole. I squirmed free of the jelly and swam in the water. I ate tiny water plants, and my head and tail grew bigger and bigger.

Young tadpoles wriggle out of the jelly.

Cousin Sally lays her eggs on land and guards them carefully. Respect to salamanders everywhere!

Spear Fishing

They call me Fearless Frog, because I'm so bold that I grin at trouble. But I'm not ~~stoopid~~ stupid! Today, like every day, I checked for footprints in the muddy bank. They show who is lurking nearby, perhaps ready to attack.

Danger Prints

Fox's four toes curve around a central pad.

Heron has three front toes.

Badger's five claws spread out when he walks.

Duck has webs between three toes.

Heron walks slowly, hardly making a ripple.

Today's prints mean Heron is nearby. There she is, on the other side of Big Pond. She stands still for ages waiting to grab her prey. I should be safe here in the waterweeds. Time for a quick nap. Zzzzz...

YIKES! A slight ripple woke me up, and there was Heron's long, sharp beak aimed straight at me! But I was quick. I made a magnificent leap to get out of the way. It'll be safer hiding in deeper water.

Big eyes for spotting small prey.

Super-sharp and very long beak!

Grey Heron

Group Birds – waterbirds

Height 1 metre

Weight 2 kilogrammes

Habitat Anywhere near fresh water, from ponds to river mouths

Food Fish, small birds and mammals, insects, crayfish, frogs (!)

Features Very long neck and legs, sharp pointed beak, can stand very still

Just in time, I hopped it!

Growing Up

Result! Heron has gone at last. While hiding, I watched the tadpoles and thought back to my own youth. I had a blobby head and scraggly tail, and I ate plants. Then changes started happening...

Here's Dragonfly crawling out of his old skin.

1. Eggs in jelly.

2. Wriggle out and swim.

Dragonfly changed shape too when he left the water to grow up. He got wings! My first change was my tail becoming big and swishy. Then, my eyes and mouth grew bigger.

3. Eat plants. Breathe with gills.

4. Eat prey. Eyes start to bulge.

5. Swim using big tail.

After a few more weeks, I felt bulges at the back of my body. Pop - out came back legs! They had been growing inside me. I could kick against the water to swim, as well as swish my tail. It felt brilliant.

Changes continued to happen! As a tiny taddy, I breathed under water using gills on either side of my head. Slowly these shrivelled away and fell off. But by then I had developed lungs inside my body to breathe air above the surface.

10. Still small, but now a fully-formed frog.

7. Tail starts to shrink.

6. Back legs appear.

8. Front legs pop out.

9. Tail almost gone. Back legs grow long and strong.

Pop - I had front legs too! At last I was a proper frog. Newt and Toad say all amphibians change their body shape. So do insects like Dragonfly. It's called mater— mutter- metamorphosis.

Netted!

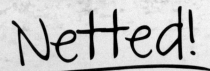

A massive hand held a straight twig.

Today I'm recovering. This is what happened: yesterday I was in the mud at the bottom of Big Pond, rooting around for juicy worms. I was swimming slowly back up to the surface, when suddenly I became trapped!

Here's me flying in mid-air!

Something lifted me out of the water. I struggled and nearly fell as I flew over the pond. Giant fingers, 100 times bigger than mine, prodded me. They felt all dry and warm. Yuck!

Suddenly I was flying again, and then I landed back in Big Pond, beside a lily pad. I was really ~~trawmaticized~~ traumatized. But nothing scares me!

The tall two-legged creatures left this page on the river bank.

Back in Big Pond. Phew!

TIPS FOR FLYING FROGS

1. Hold on tight.

2. Don't kick – you might fall out.

3. Hope for a happy landing.

TOP TIPPERS FOR
POND DIPPERS

Pond-dipping is great fun and you can learn lots about the creatures and plants who live in these mini-habitats. But beware of risks – some ponds are deep and dangerous. Take care not to harm the wildlife.

Get permission from the pond-owner and go with an experienced adult.

Stay away from steep banks and slippery or deep mud.

Stay on the bank; do not lean over too far or go into the water.

Sweep your net in a figure-of-eight shape.

Gently tip the contents of your net into pond water in a white tray, shallow white bucket or clear plastic jar to see what is there.

Make notes, draw sketches and take photos of what you find.

Carefully put back all the plants and creatures.

Replace stones, logs and other things you turn over.

Wash your hands at the end.

Moving On

Phew, it's hotting up! Summer is nearly here. Our enemies' babies are growing up, which means their parents need to find more food for them. Kingfisher is looking to catch a fish - or a small frog like me. Danger is everywhere!

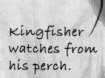

Kingfisher watches from his perch.

Old adults are bigger than me.

I'll stay out of the way on this lily pad.

This year's froglets are the smallest.

Kingfisher

Group Birds – kingfishers and bee-eaters

Length 17 centimetres

Wingspan 25 centimetres

Weight 40–50 grammes

Habitat Fresh water and riverbanks

Food Fish, water insects, shrimps, crayfish, frogs (!)

Features Long sharp beak, brightly coloured feathers. Excellent eyesight for tracking prey

We frogs and our amphibian cousins try to avoid the heat. We need to stay cool and damp, so we can breathe through our skin. If our skin goes stiff and cracked, our bodies could dry out and we might die.

Recent Catches

Here are some recent catches. One evening I caught four moths! I eat as much as I can in summer, to grow fast. It will help me survive the long, cold winter.

Cranefly

Moth

Large White Butterfly Caterpillar

Woodlouse

Some youngsters high-jump.

This one's got a free ride.

Being able to climb reeds is a useful skill.

Big Pond is shrinking in the sunshine. Time for us frogs - new little froglets and older big adults - to leave. I'm not a froglet anymore, and next year I'll be a grown-up. 'Bye Big Pond...

23

High and Dry

Big noisy beasts have destroyed Small Pond.

I could fry in that sun!

Big Pond became too hot and messy, which I hate. So I'm moving to Small Pond, where it'll be cool and damp. It's only a short hop, but I must avoid the summer sun, so I'll travel at night.

NO END TO HABITAT LOSS!

Small Pond just before the builders moved in.

Nature Expert Robin Redchest reports another bad year for wild places such as woods, heaths and especially ponds. The tall two-legged creatures fill in ponds and build massive square piles of bricks, with patches of boring grass which are no use to local animals. So each year creatures such as frogs have fewer places to feed and breed, and their numbers go down.

Disaster! Where is Small Pond? It's all changed since last year - there's no pond at all now! I'll rest on these shady pebbles for a while and then hide among some plants to avoid drying out.

Look at these empty shells of Speedy's cousins who used to live in Small Pond. They must have been too slow to escape when disaster struck. Ah, here comes Gilbert, crawling over for a chat.

Swan Mussel

Jenkin's Spire Snail

None of this was here last year!

Common Bithynia

Great Pond Snail

Gilbert can swim, fly and run. Lucky him!

Like me, Gilbert metamorphosed, but it took him two whole years to become an adult. Now he's got a hard shell with folded wings underneath. At least he can fly away to a new pond.

Great Diving Beetle

Group Insects – beetles and weevils

Length Larva 6 centimetres, adult 3.5 centimetres

Weight 3–5 grammes

Habitat Fresh water and gardens

Food Water insects and worms, small fish, tadpoles

Features Strong, sharp mouthparts to jab prey, back legs fringed with hairs for swimming. Uses reflection of moonlight to find new ponds

Last Leap

As you know by now, I like adventure more than most frogs. But yesterday evening was really not fun! It's autumn now, and I am quite cold and slow. While I was looking for somewhere to spend the night...

Sibyl is covered in hard scales.

Grass Snake

Group Reptiles – snakes and lizards

Length Female 1.6 metres, male 1.2 metres

Weight 200–300 grammes

Habitat Most places except cold, dry areas

Food Small creatures such as frogs and toads. Also fish, mice and insects

Features Long, bendy body, wide mouth, fast strike. Unlike some snakes, does not have venomous fangs

...I heard rustling, then out of the corner of my eye, saw Sibyl's big eyes and open mouth coming towards me. That snake-in-the-grass, Sibyl, was hiding among fallen leaves. Once again, I had to leap for my life. Yikes!

My great leap to safety!

My muscles are just warm enough to still work.

Each day is cooler, with less daylight. I expect warm-blooded Mouse is still racing about. But all of us cold-blooded creatures are getting ready to settle down for our Cold Sleep.

COLD SLEEP

Frogs and other amphibians are cold-blooded. Your body temperature varies with the outside temperature, so when it gets cooler in autumn, your bodies cool down too. We move about slower and, when winter comes, we stop moving altogether! We go into a deep sleep, or torpor, and don't wake up until the sun warms us up again in spring.

Frog's body temperature during Cold Sleep.

Frog's body temperature in the summer.

Ready for Winter

It's soooo gooood to be back at My Den. Luckily, no one else has moved in. I'll spend the winter here again, away from danger. It will be boring, but safe.

28 OCTOBER

AUTUMN DEN CHORES
- Check My Den for intruders and rubbish.
- Find plenty of lovely wet leaves and nice damp moss for my ~~doovay~~ duvet.
- Snuggle down into the soft moist soil.
- Cover myself with the duvet.
- Relax, stay cool and wait for spring.

This sharp thing was left in the grass.

Old leaves look so untidy.

Ouch, that hurt! Someone left a broken sharp thing in the way and now I've got a cut on my leg. Why are the tall two-legged creatures so careless? We have to cope with more and more rubbish everywhere.

This is probably my last day awake. Bare trees, low sun, long nights, frosty mornings. Time for my Cold Sleep. But first, I'll read this postcard from Stickle.

Dear Frog,

After you left Big Pond in early summer, the water got so hot that many of us couldn't breathe. I made it through, but our friend Roach didn't. You're lucky, living in water and on land. Anyway, see you next year,

Stickle Stickleback

Fearless Frog

The Old Den

Autumn Lane

F1P OND

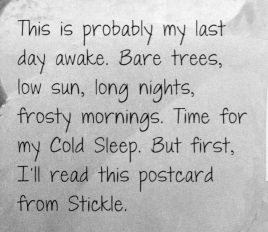

My brain is feeling sleepy.

It's been an epic year! I've survived lots of adventures and learned a lot too. Now I'll settle down in My Den, and write one last page in my diar-dia-di-d-ZZZZZZZZ.

Ouch! The sharp thing cut my leg.

What They Say About Me

My diary describes what I think of all the creatures I meet. But what do they think of me? Let's find out...

> Frog goes on about being brave, bold and ready for danger. But can Frog fly, store air for breathing underwater under its wing covers or suck the juicy insides out of a tadpole? No, Frog can't, but I can!

Great Diving Beetle

Otter →

> Frog is lively and quick in warm weather, so he's hard to catch. But I'll make a snack of him yet. I'll sneak up on him one cold day, when he's dull and drowsy and I'll gobble him up. Yes I will!

Newt

> Frog is SO boring - dreary green, sits around croaking. I'm a super flier, with brilliant feathers and an amazing lifestyle. Who would YOU rather hang out with - me or Frog?

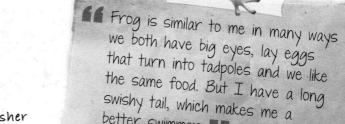

> Frog is similar to me in many ways - we both have big eyes, lay eggs that turn into tadpoles and we like the same food. But I have a long swishy tail, which makes me a better swimmer.

Kingfisher

Common Toad

> Frog leaps further than me, jumps higher, swims faster and croaks louder. His skin is more colourful. But I don't mind. I'm not jealous. Not envious at all. No, really, I'm OK...

30

Tricky Terms

Amphibian A cold-blooded animal that lives in water and on land. It spends the early part of its life as a legless larva or tadpole, then changes or metamorphoses into an adult. Frogs, toads, newts and salamanders are all amphibians.

Breed Reproduce, or mate, to make more of your own kind.

Carnivore A creature that eats mainly meat, in the form of other animals.

Cold Sleep Frog's name for a long period of inactivity during the winter. It is often called hibernation, but is more properly known as torpor.

Cold-blooded A creature that cannot make warmth inside its body, and so is usually at the same temperature as its surroundings.

Embyro An animal or plant when it has just started developing and is very tiny, young and not fully formed.

Gills Body parts for breathing underwater by taking in oxygen (as lungs do in land animals).

Habitat loss Disappearance of ponds, woods, rivers, grasslands, swamps and other natural places, usually due to the activities of people.

Metamorphosis When an animal changes greatly in body shape as it grows. For example, when a legless, tailed tadpole changes into a four-legged, tail-less frog, or a caterpillar becomes a butterfly.

Nutrients Chemicals that bodies need to stay healthy. Vitamins and minerals are nutrients.

Prey An animal that is hunted and eaten for food.

Spawn Eggs of water animals such as fish and frogs.

Tadpole The young form of an amphibian such as a frog, toad or newt, with no legs, a long tail and gills to breathe underwater.

Tall two-legged creatures The name used by Frog and other animals for humans.

Venom A harmful substance jabbed with sharp body parts – such as teeth, spines or a sting – into a victim. Venom can cause pain, inability to move or even death.

Warm-blooded A creature that can make warmth inside its body, so that it stays at a constant high temperature and can move about actively even in very cold conditions.

Grass Snake

" Frog boasts about laughing at danger, staring fear in the face and kicking threats into the long grass. I can't do that last one, so I have made up my mind to definitely catch and eat Frog - next year. "

Index